NETWORK MARKETING LIKE A PRO

SIMPLE STEPS TO GET STARTED AND BECOME A NETWORK MARKETING PRO

NEAL MARKOWITZ

CONTENTS

NETWORK MARKETING LIKE A PRO

*SIMPLE STEPS TO GET STARTED AND BECOME A
NETWORK MARKETING PRO*

NEAL MARKOWITZ

NETWORK MARKETING CONCEPT

*N*etwork **Marketing** can be expressed as a marketing strategy in which the sales force is compensated for the total sales generated by them and the people whom they have recruited. It is also known as **Multi-level marketing** (**MLM**). As we just said, marketing is done at multiple levels. Therefore, compensation is also rendered at multiple levels.

Moreover, the sales force recruited by an individual is referred to as the participant's downline. Network marketing is a network of people who have access to a range of products and services that is distributed through that network. People no longer need to operate through a shop-front. They can just buy these services or products for personal use or for selling the same to others.

As time passes and more and more people get involved, the sales and distribution of products or services also increase proportionately. Along the way, a portion of the profits on those products and services are paid to you and people in your 'down-line'. In time, the opportunity to create a regular income from a team of people using and selling products becomes a reality. Several millions of people around the globe are involved in network marketing today and this figure seems to be ever evolving.

Manufacturers, many of them Fortune 500 companies, now see it as a viable and credible alternative for distributing their products and services. Allowing customer access to products or services via outlets or using any conventional retail method is a costly affair. Moreover, it is also relatively more difficult. Today, almost everything— including health supplements, cosmetics, cleaning products, training materials, clothes, cars and travel—can be and is being sold through network marketing.

Some of the most famous names in the network marketing industry include: Avon, Usana, Melaleuca, Mary Kay, Quixtar, Herbalife, Amway, Tupperware, Juice Plus, Nu Skin and AIM. Technology, especially the Internet, has had a dramatic impact on the industry, and more and more, it is seen to be moving into the marketing mainstream. The industry is rapidly maturing and more and more professionals are becoming network marketers. So, it would not be wrong to say that network marketing has arrived and is posing to be a major force in the marketing domain.

It is an excellent way to get into business, it has several appealing aspects that cannot be found in mainstream businesses, in addition to the fact that the money earned for the effort put in is much higher than for any other comparable domain of work. Getting started could have been tough, but the fruit of labor come in the form of residual income and a steady passive stream of income.

Earlier, network marketing was, for many people, an alternative source of income. This option is still available today, but now increased numbers of people are involved in this domain. However, for some people it is an opportunity to establish a business that is, and will continue to be, their main source of income. One of the biggest mistakes made by people becoming involved with network marketing is, failing to treat it as a real business from the very beginning. Reasons like relatively low start-up cost, and a high degree of flexibility, cause most people to treat it more as a hobby.

This report aims to bring forth the different aspects of Network Marketing Business. Although, the intent, purpose and objectives of every business are different, many of the principles, fundamentals and attitudes behind making each business a success remain the same.

If you are capable of giving in the effort and time that a Network Marketing Business requires to get started and recognize that many of the principles and challenges are no different from any other business in this world, then there can be nothing stopping you. Numerous Network Marketing companies are now established all over the globe. The way they do business, their structure and the terminology used varies from company to company.

WHY NETWORK MARKETING?

The first thing to remember is you are starting a business. In this instance, the type of business you are considering is a network marketing business. Network marketing businesses each have their own opportunities and risks. They can be incredibly rewarding on many levels and as challenging as any mainstream business.

WORKING SMARTER, **not harder**

There was a time when simply working hard meant that you had the opportunity to steer ahead of the average person who perhaps had a more relaxed approach to work. In the present scenario, tables have turned. Strong work ethics remain a prerequisite even today, but it is certainly not the only thing that you shall require for a flourishing business. Success is about being smarter and often doing things differently to the way we would have done them in the past. Network marketing, allows you to do just that, while at the same time giving you the opportunity to associate with very successful people who understand this principle and who have made it work for them.

LEVERAGE AND DUPLICATION

Leverage and duplication are simply the ability to leverage your time and to duplicate your efforts. If you are working in a traditional business, your income is largely governed by the number of hours you can physically work in a week. In network marketing, as your network grows, the time collectively invested within the network is dramatically increased, and your efforts are greatly duplicated and multiplied.

Simply put, you yourself, one person, can continue to work 40 or 60 hours per week, or you can build a network where collectively, for example, 1000 people are working only 10 hours each per week, meaning your earning hours now total 10 000.You need to understand that this concept is not unique to network marketing, but is a key ingredient in most successful entrepreneurial enterprises.

Most successful entrepreneurs use it to build their wealth. If you look at people who have established large franchising businesses, you will realize that they base their success on duplication and leverage of one successful store, repeating it nationally and, ideally, globally.

PASSIVE INCOME versus active income

Active income is best described as having to continually work, trading hours for dollars, in order to maintain that income. Passive income means that, in time, you won't have to perform any physical work, but you can still maintain the income. Given the choice, most people would prefer passive income over-active income. The majority of people think of passive income in terms of the royalties paid to recording artists and authors, or the returns on investment of property owners and shareholders. Further to these are the entrepreneurial business owners who derive large passive incomes from their businesses. In some cases, passive income can be established without much effort; in other cases a certain amount of work may be required to maintain the flow of passive income.

Several different models exist. However, they are all based on the same concepts. You need to work hard now to gain tomorrow. Passive income gives the recipient's choice; they are not tied down to working hours for dollars but are in the unique position of having control over what it is they want to do with their time. Passive income provides the opportunity to have greater control of what you want to do in your day— if you feel like going to the golf course for a quick game of golf, you can go ahead with your plan; if you have some tasks lined up for the day, you can take them up; if you want to go off on a holiday on a whim, then go.

All in all, when you have a source of passive income, you have full control over your life and the independence to do whatever you want and a Network Marketing business helps you achieve just that. Many people who built successful network marketing businesses now enjoy the passive income they bring. You may need to work hard upfront, but the benefits that you will reap from the same will certainly be worth all the effort and hard work.

. . .

Low capital investment

For many of those who dream of owning their own business, a major hurdle to be overcome is the costs and risks associated with buying an existing business or setting one up in the first place, often representing hundreds of thousands of dollars and a lot of risk. One of the attractive features of building a network marketing business is the low capital, or low entry cost, which is required to get started. You don't need to spend a fortune to get started. In fact, most of the Network Marketing companies may just want you to pay for some startup costs and purchase an initial product. If a person goes on to successfully develop their network marketing business, the return on such a low initial capital investment can be significant.

Low operating cost

The ongoing operating costs required by the majority of network marketing businesses are generally very low when compared with a traditional business producing similar turnover. Costs often revolve around accessing educational and motivational material, acquiring tools for building business and attending seminars provided and organized with the intent to build a strong support system.

Further to this are incidental costs such as phone, fuel and other small home office operating costs. As the volume produced throughout the network is built on the principle of leverage and duplication of a number of independent business owners collectively establishing their own businesses and subsequent volume, the costs in achieving that volume are greatly reduced by spreading them across each independent business owner.

As a result, the operating costs of the business are rather low. There is minimalistic need for staff or infrastructure and overhead costs are also significantly curtailed.

PART-TIME COMMITMENT still works

A significant advantage of being involved in network marketing is the opportunity to establish it part-time alongside your current occupation or business. For those whose dream has been to own a business but who have feared taking the plunge due to the risk involved in giving up a secure job and income to venture into completely new and unknown territories. This aspect of business considerably reduces the risk. Traditional businesses are often associated with the owner feeling trapped and can't risk simply walking away from it, the opportunity to develop something on the side with a view that someday, it will replace their current income stream is also very attractive. After building the network marketing business part-time to a point that the income derived from it can safely replace that from the job or traditional business, one can then comfortably move into working full-time for the Network Marketing.

SUPPORT SYSTEMS

The pioneering reasons for the popularity of franchising are that people buying into a franchise do so with a sense of confidence from the fact that they have the infrastructure and process in place and they don't have to start from scratch. Network marketing also provides this sense of security. You are not all by yourself in this business. However, you are surely all for yourself in this business.

Many network marketing companies, particularly the larger ones, have a substantial support system in place to assist the business owners. In some cases these support systems are run by some of the more successful business owners and leaders from within the network, people who understand the value of sharing their experience and knowledge in order to assist their own organization grow quicker.

Another major benefit of having a support system in place is that it allows you to leverage your time all the more. You can direct your people to the support system and letting it do most of the work for you, rather than you being solely responsible for the team training and support.

Creating positive cash flow

Cash flow Quadrant, an international bestseller, by Robert Kiyosaki and Sharon Lechter, advocates Network Marketing in the strongest words and tones and highlight the importance of creating a positive cash flow for achieving wealth. Negative cash flow is the default mode of operation for most people, as they look the constantly accumulating debt on them. The majority of people run out of money before the end of each month, and 'when it's drastic, put it on plastic'.

Most of them will spend their entire lives living from month to month, heavily in debt, and as a result will never go on to achieve their goals or dreams. For the average person, once they find themselves in this position it is very difficult to turn it around, because the negative cash position makes it almost impossible to get ahead—unless, of course, they win the lottery that they are all waiting to win.

The exact reverse of this concept is positive income. So, in this case, your income will be much more than what you can spend on your living expenses. Network marketing gives a person the opportunity to establish a positive income by offering them a business that requires very little in the way of start-up and ongoing costs, something they can develop part-time with no threat to their current income and, in the big scheme of things, allows for very little or no risk.

More importantly, a network marketing business offers the potential of providing passive and exponentially growing income that in time becomes a positive cash flow because income outweighs the expenditure. They key to get the positive cash flow started is to invest your extra money in activities that can generate more positive cash flow for you. This starts a chain reaction of positive cash flow for you.

How To Create **Wealth**

If you read through experiences of people who have been successful in establishing their Network Marketing business, you will realize that they have been able to do so by recognizing the possibilities in using it as a vehicle to create a large passive income and positive Cash flow, and then using the same to create more of cash flow to increase wealth.

For many, it is not only an opportunity to create a positive cash flow, but it also allows them to know people and their stories of success in this business, which is surely a learning experience like no other. Most successful network marketing business owners have found financial independence through their network marketing business, and many have used the positive cash flow to further build wealth through investments, property or the purchase of other business ventures.

NETWORK MARKETING /MLM MODEL

&

*W*e had previously mentioned that the other name for Network Marketing is MLM or Multi-Level Marketing. It is obvious from this term is that, in this form of marketing, people are recruited at several levels to market a product or service. Therefore, a company hires people as sales representatives, affiliates or associates to perform the following tasks:

- Get customers, introduce them to the product/service and generate sales
- Introduce, recruit and train other people to work as sales representatives.

The next step is to look at how the model of Network Marketing works.

NETWORK MARKETING MODEL
The Network Marketing model's working can be demonstrated by illustrating four steps, which are as follows:

- *Step I: Customer acquisition by sales representatives*

THE FUNDAMENTAL OBJECTIVE of sales representatives, affiliates or associates, is to identify prospective customers and convert them into customers. These sales representatives are hired by the MLM Company. So, the company determines the compensation and targets for the sales representative. While many may say that the target is to get as many customers as possible, it is important to determine a quantitative value to describe targets.

THE SET TARGET must be high enough to generate substantial sales as well as low enough to ensure that the representative is able to retain these customers over the long haul. Moreover, if the company you are registered to pays more for registering more representatives to the company than getting customers, be sure to first make customers and then train them for working as representatives for the company. This is the recommended strategy of operation for companies that focus on the "duplicate yourself" plan.

- *Step II: Add more sales representatives to the company:*

ONCE YOU HAVE MADE customers and generated sales for the company in the same way, as you would have done for any other marketing method, the next step is to train your customers to work as representatives. In other words, you need to train them to not just generate sales, but also train their target customers in the same way as you are training them. The people you recruit in this manner are called 'down-line'. Here your role is of a recruiter rather than a retailer or distributor.

- ***Step III: Teaching your down-line to recruit and train others:***

AS A SALES REPRESENTATIVE, it is your responsibility to generate sales, train other sales representatives and train your sales representatives to train others. So, when you down-line has achieved sufficient sales for your company, the next step is to help them and teach them to train their customers to act as sales representatives themselves. Your purpose and objectives at this stage will again depend on the type of commission plan your company is offering. Strategize your plan to ensure that you get maximum benefits and the highest commissions.

- ***Step IV: Create a chain of marketers:***

ONCE YOU HAVE TRAINED one of your sales representatives to generate sales and recruit/train more sales representatives, it is time for you to get on to train another sales representative in the same manner as you trained the first representative. As you train more people to work, you create a level of marketers. When they train more people, they create their down-line, which is the next level of marketers. This is the essence of network marketing or multi-level marketing. In this manner, companies reach out to the maximum audience with minimum costs and in the shortest period of time.

HOW TO FIND PROSPECTS/
GENERATE LEADS

*W*HY IT'S IMPORTANT:

NETWORK MARKETING HAS two basic goals. The first of these goals is to generate sales by selling the product or service of the company to as many people as possible. However, the other goal is to motivate the customer to become an independent distributor in his or her own capacity. The attainment of both these goals requires the creation of what are called business leads or business prospects. Business leads can be created in several ways. One of the simplest ways to generate leads is to refer the product or service to friends and family. You may extend the domain of this referral to your social and professional network.

However, from the business perspective, this method may not be able to give you the kind of results that you hope to achieve. Therefore, several other tools may be used for this purpose. These tools include conducting research, holding marketing campaigns like pamphlet distribution or hold an event that directly or indirectly endorse your product or service. Similar marketing techniques exist for online multi-level marketing as well. Commonly adopted methods include squeeze pages and popups.

These methods are ways in which you can collect user information. For instance, a squeeze page gives information to the user in the form of an article or a clip. By the end of the clip or article, the user is asked to leave their credentials along with a contact detail. So, this is a way by which you can get to prospective customers who can be expected to buy your product or service in the future.

It is imperative from the discussion that your online existence can go a long way in determining how well and how many business leads you can generate. In other words, it will determine how many potential customers are within your access. Once you have the prospective audience figured out, it should not be difficult for you to offer them your products or services and share a long-term relationship with you. Summing up, the ability of a multi-level marketer to generate business leads determines his or her success in the field. So, it can play a significant role in determining your survival in a company.

Required skills:

What you are running is a small business and as a professional, you must have the required skills and trade secrets to succeed in this profession.

Therefore, your chances of achieving success largely depend on how much you are willing to educate yourself. Moreover, this shall also determine how successful you will become in making Network Marketing a residual source of income for you.

To take you forward in your strides, we have given below

a few tips for you to consider and implement. Make sure you apply ALL of the following advice to maximize your results

To BEGIN...

PEOPLE DON'T JOIN A BUSINESS – They Join YOU!

- **TIP #1**

Instead of using Network Marketing to sell your products, use it as a medium to help people. Sell your product to people who need them and never go all out about the 'you can live without it' propaganda. You will certainly earn extra points for educating your customers instead of fooling them. This is a sure shot way to success.

If you possess a website, try to give it an information-giving outlook. Create it in such a manner that it teaches your visitors about what your product does and allow them to see for themselves if the product is of any use to them. Adopt the 'online tutorial' methodology.

In addition, ensure that the information that you have put on your pamphlet or website gives a clear idea to the user about your product. When you attach value to your products and present them to your customers, rest assured that you will earn loyal and long-term customers for yourself.

- **TIP #2**

Whenever you meet a prospective customer to formally or informally introduce your product or service, be sure to ask questions and allow them to share their feelings, thoughts and experiences. This will bring you in a much better position to pitch your thoughts.

As a Network Marketer, you must build relationships and

friendships. Never move ahead with the intent to acquire another business lead.

The objective must always be to educate prospective customers by telling them what is on offer and helping them understand if they need it. Whether they should join you or not should be their own decision. It is only then that you will be able to contribute constructively to the business.

When the timing is right, the professional marketer will invite a prospect and depending on his or her situation, pitch one of the two things:

1: If it is warranted, the professional marketer may decide to invite the prospective customer to meet on a one-on-one or two-on-one basis.

2: The professional marketer may, as an alternative, invite the prospective customer for a phone call or webinar for pitching the product.

- Personal interaction is one of the most critical components when it comes to building rapport. Therefore, a professional marketer will connect to the people on a personal basis as much as possible and on a regular basis. This element is also referred to as '**Social Proof**'.
- On the other hand, be very cautious. Do not overdo it! If you take more than one hour to explain a simple business opportunity, your prospect will get bored and will conclude that working for you will be time-intensive. So, chances are less that he or she will give an affirmative response to you.

Using Different Network Marketing Tools:
Reviewing a tool is another way in which the marketer can interact with the prospect. This may involve looking at a

website or going through a magazine. On the other hand, listening to an audio/video can also be one of these methods that professional marketers may use to work for them.

- Considering the busy nature of our lives, these tools can be a great way to interact with prospects. In this way, the prospect will be educated and convinced without having to schedule any meetings of interaction sessions. It is possible that your prospect may not have the time to drive down to your office for a session, but he or she can watch a video or listen to an audio at his or her own convenience like while driving home or during a break.

If you are looking to transform your home based business into a big organization rather fast, then using this tool as a first interaction with a prospect can take you a long way in your endeavors.

This is no giving away the fact that when we are talking about Network Marketing; we are talking about a business. You must realize that network marketing is like any other business; there is no shortcut to success.

So, if you hoping to taste success, then you must be prepared to put in immense dedication and hard work on your part.

- **FINAL TIP:** Do not get into this business if you do not have the intent and desire to help others as you profit. Your profits will soar to the next level only if you have the desire to pay it forward as you cross the thresholds.

PRESENTING THE PRODUCT IN NETWORK MARKETING

HY IT'S IMPORTANT

When you interact with a prospect, the first and foremost thing that you have to keep in mind is that you are there to impart information and your role in doing this will determine the result. There are no two ways about the fact that a powerful message packed in persuasive delivery is capable of changing lives altogether. However, most people involved in MLM may have little or no knowledge of persuasive delivery or presenting techniques. So, here are a few steps that you can follow to make the best of your effort.

1. KNOW YOUR AUDIENCE: Every individual is different. So, there is no 'one presentation method' that will work for all. So, before you prepare, be sure to do a bit of research about your prospect. Also, be sure to keep the level of presentation medium. If you explain the details way too much, you may end up confusing your audience. On the other hand, not going into the details at all, you will end up making your audience go to sleep. Either way, your strategy will fall flat.

2. CONNECT: As you speak to your audience, you must listen to them and read their minds. Attempt to identify their problems and how your product is capable of helping them. Therefore, when you present your product, instead of citing all the details about your product, customize your presentation for the prospect by telling his or her how a particular detail is capable of solving one of his or her problems. In this way, you will have a better chance of striking a chord with your prospect and eventually convincing your prospect.

3.LEARN TO PRESENT AND PRACTICE IT: Speaking skills are an essential for any network marketer. In addition to many other benefits, its fundamental benefit is the remarkable boost that it gives to your confidence. The better your presentation, the more easily you will be able to influence your audience and better profits you are expected to yield. Working towards improving speaking skills is certainly an investment that will get you highest returns.

4. HANDLE DISSENTERS WELL: One of the major problems network marketers face is to deal with prospective customers, who doubt you for all you say and all you are attempting to tell them. In such cases, more often than not, you may end up getting into an argument and feel cornered if you are presenting to a group of people. Whenever such a situation arises, try to turn the situation in such a manner that your audience seems right from every perspective and you accept it.

5.DON'T JUST TELL, SHOW IT: How about I tell you all about this dress from its color to its dimensions and fabric, but do not show the same to you? Would you buy it from me? You wouldn't! In fact nobody would! It is easier to trust things or products that are present in front of you. So, as a presenter, never make the mistake of not presenting the physical product to your audience. This is the most negative thing that you can do to your presentation. Also, it will be beneficial for you to carry along the brochures, manuals or any documentation that the company has given along with the product.

6.BE FRIENDLY: Trust leads to credibility and you have a better chance of striking a deal if your prospect likes you or is comfortable with you. In order to build that kind of rapport, you need to put your guard down and show your prospects the real you. Do not be afraid of talking about your family or friends. In this way, your prospects will identify you in a more personal and relatable manner.

7. GET THE STORY ANGLE IN: Most presenters fall in the trap of going on and on about their product, its features and how what works. However, you must understand that this may sound interesting to someone who has had a first experience with the product. For someone who is yet to get his or her hands on your product, this may not sound like a favorable proposition and you will lose your prospect right away. As far as lead-ins are concerned, your prospects are interested in knowing the results and outcomes. So, as part of your presentation, you must tell them stories about user experiences instead of going all over the place with facts.

8. MAKE THEM LAUGH: If you have had the opportunity to sit in a presentation, you will agree that it is rather easy to get bored and go to sleep. As a presenter, the one weapon that you have to keep your audience from sleeping and get their attention focused on you is humor. Moreover, laughter is also a way in which your audience will become more comfortable with you, building the right foundation for a good rapport.

9.DON'T TELL – ASK: You just have to get your prospects involved in the conversation and make them feel that they are the most important. You can achieve this by asking them questions. Rather than saying "Did you know that only 1% of people retire financially free?" Ask them "Do you have any idea about what percentage of retire financially free?" If you time your questions correctly and ask the right questions, you may actually compel your prospect into a buy without having to state the same in words.

10.CITE REASONS WHY YOUR AUDIENCE MUST ACT NOW: Like we said, network marketers are not trained sales people. Therefore, they may give an awesome presentation, but take it all away by not asking for orders in the end. You have presented the prospect, told him or her why he or she needs your product and done all the things right. Now, it is time to ask for your reward. You can compel your prospect to place an order right away by giving him or her reasons for doing so. For instance, a promotional offer or a day-offer can work well for you. Anything that will force them to take a decision now is your pick.

INVITING THE PROSPECT IN NETWORK MARKETING

WHY IT'S IMPORTANT

A vital skill in network marketing is learning how to invite prospects to take a gander at your product or business opportunity. The purpose of inviting is to ask your prospect to review information that can help them achieve what they've stated they need, want, or don't want. And the invitation should always be done on the phone, not face to face where your prospects can bombard you with question after question. The more you say, the more they can say no to.

In network marketing, you're inviting people to look at either the business or the product or both.

Steps to invite the prospects to present your product:

Professional Marketing Invitation includes eight steps, which are as follows:

Step 1: Show Urgency!

It is human tendency to get attracted to people who have something or the other going on. So, sense of urgency can set the tone of your presentation.

In other words, you need to show your prospect that you

are a busy person and that you are really short on time. However, do not let this sense of urgency interfere with the way you present. Be quick, but be passionate!

- **Step 2: Compliment the Prospect!**

There is no doubt about the fact that this step is critical in view of the fact that it may actually win the deal for you. In fact, it is a major step towards building rapport with your prospect. When you give a sincere compliment to your prospect, he or she is more likely to become agreeable to you. However, be sure that the complement is not apparently fake or insincere.

Warm-Market Prospects Examples:

"I respect your success and the way you do business."

Or,

"For the time that we have known each other, I have believed that you are truly the best at your work."

The statements given above are just examples of how you can compliment your prospect. These are plain guidelines and you must use your sense of observation to find a sincere compliment for your prospect.

Starting out with conversing that you are busy and complimenting your prospect sets a positive tone for the meeting. From here on, it shall be rather tough for your prospect to act negatively towards you. Also, nowadays people rarely get compliments because of the busy nature of our lives, and they become all the more receptive to you after you your words of admiration.

An efficient network marketer always uses honest compliments to set a positive mood in the prospect.

- **Step 3: Make the Invitation!**

Invitation can be given to the prospect using one of the following methods:

- **The Direct Approach**

The direct approach is used when you are inviting people to learn more about an opportunity for them. Here are a few examples.

"Do you think a side-project will interest you if it didn't affect your current project's results?"

- **The Indirect Approach**

This is a powerful tool that is most effectively used for people who show resistance. So, actually, you ask for their help or advice on some matter and play on their ego to achieve your objective.

Examples for your Warm-Market Prospects: "I just found a business I am totally interested in, but I am not sure.

You have loads of experience behind you. Would you help me in taking a call by going through this?

OR

"I was told by a friend that I can take the right decision only if I consult a few of my most trusted friends about this business. Do you think you can help me?"

For a Cold Market: "My Company is planning an expansion in your locality. Would you do me a favor and take a look at it and let me know if you think it would work where you live"?

OR

"I have got into this business that I believe is really good. I just thought I would consult you and take your inputs. Would you be interested in taking a look at this and share your opinion on this with me?

- **The Super Indirect Approach**

The third and the last approach discussed here is the super indirect approach. It is excessively powerful owing to the fact that it is capable of working at more than one psychological level. Using this approach, you converse to the prospect that he or she is not a prospect and asks him or her to tell you about someone who may be looking for such a solution.

Examples for your Warm-Market Prospects: "Do you know someone who is looking for a work-from-home business option?"

More often than not, the prospect will not give you names. Instead, he or she will show willingness to know more about the business. The curiosity is proof enough that he or she is interested, but they will not admit it until they are fully convinced of it.

The same approach can be utilized for cold markets as

well. You can make the desired variations to the scripts to bring in the right tone and the use of words.

Step 4: If I..., Would You...?

If there is a trade secret of network marketing, then this step is surely one of them. "If I gave you a website address, will you check it out in your free time? This is a powerful question for the following reasons:

First –

This question exploits the principle of reciprocity. When you tell someone that you are going to do something for him or her, they are inevitably forced in the feeling to reciprocate your favor. So, they will do something in return for you. As humans, we are programmed for such a response.

Secondly –

When you use such a statement, you become the center of power, the controller. So, you are not asking for anything. Instead, you are asking for something in return for something.

And Third –

It immediately puts your offering forward. You, in a way, said that you are willing to do something, but the same will not happen unless you get the desired value.

- **Step 5: Confirmation #1 – Get the Time Commitment**

We have already discussed the classic case of: "If I, Would you?" Assuming you get an affirmative response to this question, it is your responsibility to seal the deal by asking for a time commitment. Given below are a few scripts that can work well for you:

"When do you think you will have the time to have a look at the website?"

Please note here that you must not suggest them on when

they should do the task. Just ask them and let them give you an answer. When you pose such a question, you allow them the freedom to think about their commitments, schedules and your offerings. In this manner, you will be able to earn a real prospect for yourself.

OR

"When do you think you could watch the presentation on the website for sure?"

If your prospect thinks and tells you that he or she will be able to see it by the weekend, go ahead and ask, "Will it be okay if I call you on Monday? You would have had a look at the website by then, right?" On the other hand, if the person said that he will be able to look at the website by Monday morning, be sure to ask, "If I called you by Monday evening, you would have had a look by then, right?" You frame a sentence similar to the ones written above depending on the response that you get from your prospect.

In response to your second question, you may get a yes or the prospect may adjust the time or date. Either case, you now have a time commitment from your prospect. So, the chances of follow through are rather high.

The point that you must note here that your prospect has set an appointment with you, and it is not the other way around.

- **Step 7:Confirmation #3 – Schedule the Next Call**

This is the simplest of all steps. You just need to ask your prospect for a time and date that is deemed suitable by him or her to talk to you. In all probability, you will get a response from your prospect. So, you have a real appointment set now. Don't forget to make the call and be punctual!

- **Step 8: Say Goodbye!**

Like we said in step 1, you must show that you are in a hurry. So, as soon as you have sealed the deal and fixed an appointment, it is time for you to get going. End it with a statement like, "Great, we'll talk then, Got to run!"

FOLLOWING UP IN NETWORK MARKETING

WHY IT'S IMPORTANT:

- Following up is significantly important for cultivating relationships and transforming prospects into customers. This is why all successful network marketers are experts at following up. As you learn to follow up, you will know how it is the base of a flourishing relationship.

- Has the prospect told you that he or she is not interested? If not, then you can still follow up. The experience and stories of many network marketers reveal that they have hardly sealed any deal in the very first contact. Moreover, it takes as many as 8-10 contacts to get to a concluding point. So, learning to follow up is plainly essential for any network marketer.

- However, in the event that you get a straightforward no from your prospect, it is a good strategy to ask your prospect if he or she will be fine with you calling him or her at a later time to see if he or she has changed mind. In all probability, your prospect will say yes to this, in which case, it is good to ask for a time as to when you should make a follow up call.

- The follow up call gives you the space and time to showcase the benefits of your offerings.

When you had contacted the prospect first, he or she may not have the requirement for your offer. However, with time, such a need may have arrived. Moreover, mentioning benefits is good in light of the fact that your mentioning of the benefits may make the prospect realize that he or she actually needs such an offer. So, the only way you will ever know if your prospect has changed his or her mind or not is by following up.

❖❖

What if your prospect tells you to not call him or her again? Well, divert from the offer and talk about the other things in your prospect's life like career, friends and family. You never know when and how you may find the plan B that you have been looking for. However, you will be able to act on your purpose and fulfill your objective only if you work and see yourself as the problem solver.

There are several techniques that you can adopt for following up. Some of these techniques include:

- **Sending an email** – Asking for email addresses from your prospects is a good practice. Also, make it a point to ask them if you sent them a follow-up email. Autoresponder *service* like AWeber or Getresponse may also be used for this purpose. These services allow you to setup automated email systems, which can be configured to send emails at regular time intervals. However, before to do this, seek their permissions because if you don't, you may actually end up ruining your relationship instead of making up.

- **Placing a phone call – You can call up your prospect after regular time intervals to ask if he or she is interested. However, if they tell you that they are not interested, be sure to ask them if it will be okay for you to call at a later time.**

- If you are new and do not have lots of leads coming in daily, follow up until the person gives you an answer! Work your leads with posture, but don't be annoying. This is how I work my follow ups.

- **First Call:** Hi Cindy, This is Debra. We had an appointment to speak at 6:00pm today. I wanted to keep my word and follow up with you at the time we agreed on. Call me back at your earliest convenience. My number is xxx-xxx-xxxx. Looking forward to speaking with you.

- **Second Call: (1 day later)** Hi John, This is Tom Doherty. We had an appointment to speak yesterday at 6:00pm. I left you a message and didn't hear back. Hope everything is all right. My call back number is xxx-xxx-xxxx. Looking forward to speaking with you.

- **Third Call: (3-5 days later)** Hi John, This is Tom Doherty. I am not sure what happened to you. I left you a few messages and have not heard back. Hope everything is all right on your end. My call back number is xxx-xxx-xxxx. Looking forward to speaking with you.

- **Fourth Call: (1 Month Later)** Hi John, This is Tom Doherty. Thought about you today, how are things? I left you a few messages and have not

heard back. Hope everything is all right on your
end. My call back number is xxx-xxx-xxxx.
Looking forward to speaking with you.

These follow up messages are just some examples.

Keep calling the prospect once a month till you hear from
them! Continue to make new contacts while you are doing
this and keep adding follow-ups to your calendar.

It is a good practice to follow up. However, be sure to ask
your prospects about when it will be possible for them to
give you feedback or response. A follow-up is crucial to your
relationship with your prospect, but this will be effective
only if you put your prospect's needs ahead of your own.

HELPING YOUR DOWNLINE TO GET STARTED

In order to help your downline get started, to get them to exhibit confidence, cheerfulness, and discipline requires you to do two things – help them gain effectiveness with MLM training and show them how it is in their best interest to do it.

MLM Training – The Key To effective Network Marketing

If you want your downline to generate business for you, you need to train them for the same. It is truly as simple as this. However, it is important to understand that the efficacy of MLM training is not dependent on how well you conduct it, but on how well the prospect absorbs it.

Training Essentials

Here are some of the things that any downline must be trained for.

- Know what is required to be effective
- Goals establishment
- Responding to people on phone calls
- Procedures and sequences for sponsoring people

- Promoting knowledge
- Presenting offers (products or services)
- Selling your offers (products or services)
- Setting appointments
- Training new distributors

The productivity of your downline increases as they become effective in one of the areas specified above. As downline prospects are able to gain their expertise on each of these areas, they will be motivated because they are effective. They will become more productivity because now they feel they can become more productive.

In addition, there are some other keys to success as well. These include:

DO follow the leader and respond to training. It is important for you to understand that you can expect to gain success at training your downline only if you are coachable downline yourself. You need to be in the business all the time and look at what the achievers are doing. Follow their footsteps to replicate their success. If you feel like, you can call your upline for advice and listen to all that he or she has to say about training your downline. This is an obvious advice, but people tend to forget it way too often. Your leaders are your richest resource. Make use of their experiences to carve out your success.

DO always sponsor. Most people fall in the trap of getting started in full throttle and then ending up stuck in the "management mode." Sponsoring people allows you to model the training process for your downlines. It is the responsibility of leaders to give a chance to new people and keep the energy in the system flowing. So, keep the zest up, always be on the look out for prospects and people interested in your business and more than anything keep interacting with new people. Keep on sponsoring!

*DON'T **abandon people.*** This is another trap that many people fall into. We have a tendency to go all guns blazing towards our target and as soon as we achieve it, we forget all about it and move on to the next. Similarly, here people tend to invest all their energies and resources into convincing a prospect and as soon as they receive that magical yes, they leave them there and go on the lookout for a new prospect. This is a particularly bad practice in view of the fact that you may not be able to build lasting relationships with your downlines. Sit down with your new distributor and help them get started right.

*DON'T **work with the wrong people.*** So, you are all sorted. You convinced your prospects, made them downlines, trained them and now they are all working effectively for you. Now, what next? Many people tend to make the mistake of handing over all the hard work and put in to someone who they believe needs it more than them. In all probability, this chosen one is usually someone who is away from all the action and this decision starts a struggle of a new kind. You may end up losing momentum and hold of your business.

Ethical behavior. If you wish to be followed, you must understand that people follow only those leaders who are known to be honest and ethical.

Boldness. Some people consider boldness, a quality of a leader and therefore, people like to follow leaders who are capable of taking bold decisions and who are bold in their mannerisms and personality. This may want you to question: what is it that I need to become bold? What are people looking for in me when they are looking for boldness? People are simply looking at your skills at work and abilities to tackle your fears. So, you must show them that you are a productive worker yourself and have the ability to handle the trickiest of situations in your own capacity.

Be interested. It is important for you to show your

downlines that their goals are of interest to you. Put your front line's goals on you & them to see. Also, make it a point to speak to them and discuss with their goals and how their efforts to achieve the same are going. This is exactly where "make it in their interest to do it" comes in.

Be an information source. Considering the fact that people are looking up to you, it is important for you to be informed about the latest in your field. Therefore, be in line with the sources. Also, be sure to reveal your sources to your downlines. This will help them become independent and you will not have to do this job forever.

Following these steps will allow you to improve their efficacy and motivate them to achieve desired results. Pumping them up is a shallow way of motivating them and may not work.

PROMOTING THE EVENTS

⁓

hat's An Event?
To be successful in network marketing, you must master how to promote events. Most people underestimate the power of events and their businesses suffer as a result. In order to understand the importance of events, you should know what is considered to be an event.

An event is any type of conference call, presentation, training, webinar or gathering of representatives that is bigger than you. Events allow prospects to see more of the company and opportunity.

Why to Promote Events?

One of the reasons to promote events is to give people the chance to see the bigger picture. If they meet with you alone or with you and another rep, they don't really know how big the opportunity is. They don't fully understand the impact that the business has made on the lives of other people.

They certainly don't yet fully understand what the business can do for them, so you have to get them to attend an event. The best way to get them to attend is to promote the event

How To Promote Events

Learning how to promote events is a requirement of a successful Network Marketing career. One of the key elements of promoting events is using "fear of loss." Keep in mind; people will always do more for what they stand to lose versus what they stand to gain.

Incorporate statements such as "This is a one time opportunity for you to meet...", "I don't know when there will be another meeting like this", "I'm not even sure I can get you on the guest list." You must make the event worthy of their time by promoting and make it sound like it is a once in a lifetime opportunity.

In order to achieve success in Network Marketing, you must try this. All top earners here are master promoters.

Teach Your Team How To Promote Events

Once you learn how to promote events, you must next teach your team members how to promote events. It's not enough that you are the only promoter. You also have to get your team to do the same; that's the only way you're going to create massive momentum in your business. Teach your team the power of fear of loss and also words that move people to action.

Instruct them to incorporate phrases such as "One time event", "I only have two VIP seats left", "Only a select group of people are being added to the guest list." These are phrases that make people change their plans, commit to attending and then actually show up.

There is a popular quote in the Network Marketing world, which says, "**One meeting must lead to another!**"

In any of your efforts to interact with the prospect, whether through webinars or calls, is not to sign someone up or sell a product, it is to get the person you are speaking to, involved in your conversation.

Many Network marketers struck gold when they got this principle working in their systems. They made some good money in the process. The secret is to just get the prospect involved in your offer to the degree that he or she will agree to meet you for another round of talks.

However, in order to take your Network Marketing business farther and higher, you must learn a very important skill: business promotion!

If there is one skill that most top people have mastered to perfection, then it is undoubtedly promotion. They simply know the fact that if they want people to turn up at their next event; they have to do something that ensures that people are excited about their next event.

To help you master this skill, we present to you some advice that you can try and test to promote your next event.

1. You can't expect the world to know about what is going on when your own team does not have the slightest idea about the same. Be sure to communicate all the details to your team. Also, it is critical for you to know that a random mail is not enough communication. You must communicate your plans on a one-to-one basis and if required, over the phone.

2. Now that you know that team needs to be informed, also understand that all of your team members need to be involved. Involving team members ensures that each one of them considers the event as his or her own and work collectively to make it a success. The more, the merrier!

3. In your attempt to maintain communication

between team members, publish updates to them on a daily basis.

4. Organize team events like fun activities to set the mood of collective responsibility and collective gains in.

5. Never go all out to perform a big event. Let small events be organized, which may eventually lead up to the big event. In this manner, you will be able to generate a good amount of excitement in the crowd, conversing with them as to why they must come to the main event in a fun way.

6. Considering the amount of stress that comes with organizing a big event, it is easy to become negative and the energy may consequently drop. Don't let such thoughts affect you.

7. One needs to keep health good.

MEASURING MULTILEVEL
MARKETING PERFORMANCE

*I*n order to analyze if a Network Marketing campaign is successful or not and if yes, how effective the same is, it is most critical to measure the performance of the team involved in multi-level marketing. Any firm's profitability is impacted by several key performance indicators. These indicators can be seen as control points, which reflect the progress and performance of the multi-level marketing team.

Moreover, they also reflect the impact of the multi-level marketing team on the business, in entirety. The Network Marketing scenario and the associated compensation plans that are offered by companies are usually very complex in nature. As a result, companies do not feel the need or are willing to spend the effort to evaluate team's performance and how the same affects the performance.

There is no doubt about the fact that the Network Marketing business is hugely impacted by the performance of the multi-level marketing team. So, why do you need to assess team performance? How can it help you? Assessing team performance provides results that can be used to formulate strategies and update business plans for the future. So, from now on, you can invest more in areas that either require your attention or are promising areas for investment.

Coming to the next important question. How can the performance of the multi-level marketing team assessed? How can you gain a quantitative analysis of results, which can be later used for planning business strategy and plan? Lastly, what are the key indicators that we mentioned previously in view of the fact that key indicators are the main evaluators of team performance?

Some of the parameters that can be used for assessing performance are to see if the members of the team achieved their targets and the cumulative sales targets that were set for them. In addition, parameters like the number of recruits added, sales margins, cost benefit analysis for the business and customer satisfaction are good evaluators to see and consider. All of these results can be used for formulating strategies and plans for the future. In fact, several companies use these parameters, as their basis for future plans and strategies.

The other facet of this evaluation is to consider business targets. Companies and management tend to set unrealistic targets that seem impossible to achieve. Lastly, it is not possible to evaluate the performance unless you have had a look at the compensation plan offered to the representative. For instance, if your team is unable to retain distributors, instead of penalizing them, have a look at the compensation plan and revise the same. In addition, you must also understand that external factors like demand shortfall and economic down turn come into play. These factors are beyond anybody's control. Therefore, longevity can be achieved only after team performance has been evaluated and corrective measures have been introduced for loopholes.

HOW TO DEVELOP A
COMPENSATION PLAN

＊

WHY IT'S IMPORTANT
We have already described that multi-level marketing or network marketing is a business model that uses a network of independent distributors to present the products or services to the customers or end users. In order to pay multi-level marketers, a multi-level commission plan must also be devised. You must also ponder a thought on the fact that marketers hire marketers and form a chain. So, a payment plan is much more complex than the ones put in place for normal businesses. Moreover, pay plan is the key driving force to influence the direction of results. Therefore, commission plans can be good way to reap profits.

- **Basic Compensation Strategy**

EVERY COMPANY HAS A DIFFERENT STRUCTURE. Moreover, the commission plans set for the business also differ; some of which may be extremely complex as well. However, you must keep in mind that the basic compensation strategy for all such compensation plans remains the same.

- *Retail Commission:*

The meaning of this term is understandable from the very term 'retail commission' and refers to the commission that is given to the marketer by the company on generated sales. The more the sales, the higher is the commission. In other words, this commission also acts as an incentive for the individual marketer to work hard and generate leads for the business.

- *Sponsor Commission:*

A MARKETER GENERATES sales at two levels. The marketer himself does the first level of generating sales. The commission paid for this level of sales is called retail commission. The second level at which a marketer generates sales is in the form of sales that the marketer's downlines generate. The commission given for these sales is called sponsor commission. Companies that focus their compensation plans around increasing distributor base tend to pay higher sponsor commission.

- *Training Commission:*

This is the third category of commission that is paid by companies to marketers specifically for training their downlines. Marketers are given this commission have the experience and knowledge to become leaders.

Leveraged income is the most important aspect of MLM.

In other words, a marketer doesn't just earn for his efforts by selling products or services, but he or she also earns for the sales generated by his or her downlines. It is important to mention here that some companies create complex compensation plans, which may take unethical paths for fooling the marketer. Beware of such MLM companies.

Different Types of Plans

There are many different varieties of compensation plans offered by Network Marketing companies. But they tend to be variations on four major types of plans...

THE UNILEVEL PLAN

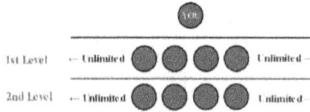

THIS IS the most basic and most easily explained multi-level marketing compensation plan. The first level indicates the downlines that you recruit. However, the next level shows the downlines of your downlines and the network forms, level after level. However, your company shall not pay you for the complete chain. They set a limit to the number of levels you will be paid for. Typically, companies pay till the sixth or seventh level only.

PROS: Simple, easy to explain
CONS: Lack of flexibility

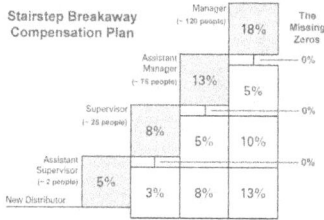

The Stairstep Breakaway Plan

This plan is the same as the unilever plan. However, in this case, once a marketer breaks through the threshold performance level, he or she can advance to the higher level. In this way, he or she can break away from the sponsor line to which he or she belongs. It is important to mention here that the original sponsor shall continue to receive commission on sales by the sponsor line.

PROS: Key benefits of this plan are that it is driven by performance and volume of work. Therefore, they are easily modifiable and are an accepted plan by several regulatory agencies.

CONS: The fundamental con of this plan is that it is complex and difficult to comprehend. Moreover, it promotes inventory uploading and requires high purchase volume.

The Matrix Plan

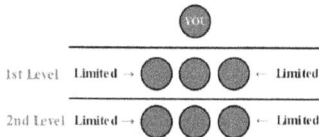

This grid-type plan and each of the levels of the plan are

limited to a certain width. For instance, if you have a 3x5 matrix, then depth of 5 levels is allowed and each level can have only 3 downlines.

So, what do you do if one level is fully filled up and you have a new sponsor? You go to the next level and fit it in there. The next level can be used until it fills up and you then move to the next level. This is perhaps the reason why you will notice that in some places, this plan is also called forced matrix plan.

If you get in on the first levels of your sponsor's matrix, and they personally sponsor a lot of people then, you might get some "spill-over" or people who are under you. Some commonly used configurations include 3x8 and 2x2.

PROS: Opportunity for "spill-over"

CONS: Attracts loafers or "dead weight"

Other names of this plan include "socialist" or "welfare" matrix. In some cases, one downline may have another downline under it. So, some people may be earning commissions from people while they may not be doing anything at all for them.

Binary Plan

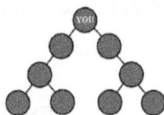

In the plan shown above, each new downline can be placed in one of the two legs of the binary tree. The same holds true for all the downlines, resulting in the creation of a matrix series. There is no depth limit on payment, but there is usually a finite amount that can be paid out for.

PROS: The advantages of using this plan include simplicity, unlimited depth support and the fact that this model promotes group cooperation.

CONS: The disadvantages of this plan include legal issues and the need for it to be balanced at each leg of the plan.

VARIATIONS / ADDITIONS

Following are some network marketing compensation plan variations that are out there today.

Fast-Start Bonus

Fast-Cash or Fast-Start bonus is a payment scheme, which allows distribution of incentives to people for sponsoring on a personal basis. These incentives can be as low as $20 and as high as $200. As this is a method used by the pyramid scheme, the FTC does not consider this method of making money, which only involves the marketer in signing up people, legal. However, companies for a quick start use this strategy whether they wish to get started with recruitment of downlines.

Infinity Bonus

This plan is an additional bonus plan that is based on the volume of the organization. Typically, this may amount to 1-2% additional bonus to the marketers. This may sound like a small amount to you and will not take a substantial turn until the organization becomes large enough. Moreover, an extra 1-2% per month is certainly a decent addition. This bonus is capable of doing two things for you.

1. This commission is made keeping the whole organization in mind.
2. This commission also ensures that you use the online help and support to provide the downlines.

You must have a look at the compensation structure that your company is offering to know how and when you, as a downline, can be blocked. For instance, if someone in your downline achieves the eligibility and requirements for the infinity bonus, you may be blocked out because same bonus cannot be given to two downlines belonging to the same downline. Fortunately, you will still be eligible for the normal compensation. In addition, when you have an organization large enough to get infinity bonus, you will already be earning a large amount of money to support this eligibility.

Roll-up/Compression

As a situation that is known to commonly occur with any organization, don't be surprised if you have people in your downline who are not performing or buying any products or services. In order to deal with such a situation, companies have what is called compression or roll-up. So, if you have a downline who hasn't purchased anything for more than a month, you must roll-up and allow the downline on the next level to come up to a higher level.

It is typical of network marketing plans to pay less to the marketers of the lower level. So, rolling up allows you to get your best performing distributors at the higher level. The fact that they get a higher commission than others and perform better than others keeps the system effective and continually working towards performing better. Just as is the case with infinity bonus, compression may not be significant until your organization is significantly large.

MATCHING

Matching or Mega-matching is another type of binary MLM compensation plan. In the binary plan, you, as the sponsor, get paid for the downlines in each leg that follows you. It is immaterial whether you or someone else sponsored the downline. However, in this case, matching is done to check if you had personally sponsored the downline or not.

COMPARISON OF NETWORK MARKETING AND TRADITIONAL MARKETING

*M*any people advocate the use of Network Marketing and indicate that it is much more effective than the traditional counterpart when it comes to leads generation. However, for people who are already running their business using the traditional strategies, this shift is a difficult and risky one. To add to the misery, the differences between the two methodologies are not apparent to many people, which make it difficult for them to make a decision. Here we have dedicated this chapter to explore the difference between these strategies. The following sections illustrate these differences.

DIFFERENCE BETWEEN NETWORK and Traditional Marketing

One of the most significant and crucial differences between the two types of marketing strategies is the marketer role. Multi-level marketing starts like any other traditional marketing technique in the sense that the company hires a sales representative and pays it for promoting and distributing its products or services.

However, the role of the marketer varies in MLM when the sales representative is also expected to hire more representatives under him or her to generate business leads.

- Under Network Marketing, a marketer is responsible for getting and increasing customers, in addition to hiring new sales representatives. On the other hand, a marketer of the traditional marketing approach does not have the right to hire sales representatives.
- In traditional marketing methods, the financial arrangement of the company determines the number of sales representatives that the company can hire. However, in case of network marketing, there is no limit on the number of sales representatives that can be hired. However, there is certainly a limit on the sales representatives that can be hired by one sales representative.
- The direction of expansion of the marketing network is typically horizontal for a traditional marketing company. However, the same for a MLM company is vertical in nature.
- Another level of difference between the two types of marketing companies lies in the manner in which sales representatives are compensated. MLM companies follow the commission plan and sales representatives are paid on a performance basis. On the other hand, traditional marketing companies pay fixed salaries to their representatives. This is the reason why unlimited representatives can be hired by MLM, but only traditional marketing companies can hire a limited number of representatives.
- Investments and startup costs for MLM companies

are lesser than traditional marketing companies as for traditional marketing companies; the whole distribution channel must be set up beforehand.

- In traditional marketing companies, the performance of a single manager can affect the performance of the company significantly. On the other hand, even if a sales representative does not perform, but the whole group performs, the MLM Company is sure to earn profits.
- The rise and promotion of representatives through the organizational ladder in MLM companies are purely performance-based. On the other hand, traditional marketing companies go through tedious appraisal, hiring and firing process for the same.

The points mentioned above clearly indicate how MLM is better than traditional marketing, particularly pointing out to MLM's flexibility and susceptibility to growth.

IMPROVING SKILLS FOR NETWORK MARKETING

❧

*H*ere we will discuss a few guidelines that will help you improve your skills as a network marketer. Before anything else, it is important for the marketer to understand that you may be endorsing a brilliant company with a perfect product or service, but you will still need to put in immense amount of hard work and dedication if you wish to gain any success in your endeavor. You cannot sit back and wait for things to happen. The following tips help you improve your multi-level marketing skills.

- *Managing your downline:*

Your main source of income is your downline. In addition, he or she is also your biggest asset. So, if you wish to get more returns, you must manage your downlines well and motivate them to work hard to maximize sales.

- *Understanding different people:*

As a marketer, you can expect to work with diverse

people, coming from different backgrounds. Therefore, you may need to train yourself to identify their strengths and weaknesses and use this information to customize your training and motivation schedule for them.

- *Be positive and accept rejection:*

Rejection rate is significantly high in Network Marketing. So, it is important to stay positive.

- *Be persistent:*

Some people tend to lose interest quickly if they think their plans are not working up to the mark. This must be avoided completely.

- *Undertake constant research:*

REMEMBER that you are out there to sell a product that belongs to a company. You cannot expect to make any substantial progress here unless you enter the arena with all the facts on the tips of your fingers.

- *Be on a constant path of learning:*

No matter how good you are, you are still learning and there is always that room for improvement. So, keep learning and remain updated about the happening around you.

- *Work on your communication skills:*

Effective communication and selling skills are keys for

the success of every marketer. Therefore, constant practice of developing communication skills is required on your part.

- *Be reliable:*

Reliability is the foundation of trust. Unless a person finds you reliable, chances are that he or she will not trust you. Moreover, as a marketer, you are representing a company and its products or services. So, act responsibly and furnish only correct information. Use of unethical ways to generate leads is practice you must keep away from.

NETWORK MARKETING BUSINESS ESSENTIALS

*ou must have heard of many MLM companies that opened up and then closed down in no time. As a rule, this business sees many companies open up and shut down with time. Therefore, long-term existence of a company is something that only the fortunate and talented see. Try to find out the names of MLM companies that are successful. Also, observe the common and striking characteristics of such companies. Lastly and most importantly, evaluate how the company for achieving success uses MLM strategies? Here are some of highlights of a top-performing multi-level marketing company.

- *Unique Product:*

It is important for you to understand that even the best sales force and marketing plan cannot sell a product that possesses no value. In other words, you need a product that is unique and useful or relevant to a customer. You may be big, but unless you have a product that can strike a chord with your target customers, success will remain a distant dream.

- *Stability:*

If there is one trait that determines the endurance and longevity, it is certainly stability. If a company is well established, it is highly unlikely for short-term financial setbacks to affect it. Moreover, most companies have elaborate plans and strategies planned out to ensure long-term stability. You can question the stability of an organization if it has a history of changing individuals at important positions.

- *Financial Strength:*

ANOTHER COMPONENT that plays an equally important role in determining an organization's stability is financial strength. Therefore, before a company decides to explore the MLM option, it should ensure that they would benefit from MLM and possess the resources to invest in such a venture.

- *Training of Members and Support*

If you look at any MLM company that is known to be performing well on a consistent basis, you will realize that its high performance is backed with training and support. Distributors of a company are the cores of its marketing campaign. Therefore, it is their responsibility to educate and train them for withstanding the turmoil of the marketing business. Training is usually imparted in the form of conferences or webinars. In addition to this, companies also provide support to their distributors in the form of live chat and hotlines to resolve their queries.

- **Business Building Tools**

It is not possible for any company to succeed without the support of its marketers. This is perhaps the reason why companies provide business-building tools to their distributors. Some of the commonly used tools include diaries, planners, ecards, tester and relationship management systems.

- **Compensation Plan**

The biggest asset of any MLM company is its marketing force and there is no better way to show gratitude towards their efforts than giving them a compensation plan that they deserve. Therefore, it is the responsibilities of the company to devise a balanced compensation plan that can benefit the financial resource plan of the company and keep the marketers happy.

ADVANTAGES OF NETWORK *Marketing*

THERE ARE several benefits of using multi-level marketing, which are discussed in detail below.

- **Minimum Entry Barriers:**

THE BIGGEST ADVANTAGE that network marketing offers is that it is fairly simple to get into this business. The eligibility requirements to enter and make it big in this domain of work are not difficult or too high. Simply, you don't need a degree or years of experience to get into Network Marketing. All that you need is the will to succeed and the attitude to work hard and dedicate yourself to your purpose.

- *Financial Flexibility:*

THE FINANCIAL REQUIREMENTS of the Network Marketing business at the start-up level are rather low. Actual costs differ from company to company. While some company may require you to pay for registration and start-up kit, others may demand a monthly investment from you.

- *Demands focused efforts:*

A NETWORK MARKETER needs to solely focus all his or her efforts towards marketing the product or service and recruiting more representatives for the company. All the rest is done by the company itself that is you are only marketing an already manufactured product and once you make a sale, all issues regarding shipping the product to the customer and maintaining records can be left to the company to resolve.

- *Flexible Hours:*

WORK HOURS FLEXIBILITY is a major advantage of working as a network marketer. You can work according to your will and convenience. Moreover, there is no restriction for you to work full-time or part-time. You can work whenever you like and from wherever you like.

- *Network Marketing offers Leveraged Income:*

ONCE YOU HAVE CREATED enough business leads and manu-factured a solid downline for yourself, you can rest assured. You will have residual monthly income without having to do anything yourself. Your downlines will earn for you.

- *Pre-Existing Systems*

LIKE WE HAVE MENTIONED time and again, you need to hire and train representatives for your company. However, you don't need to worry about how you need to go about the training process. There are set procedures to follow, which the company will share with you.

- *Personal Growth and Development:*

AS A NETWORK MARKETER, you constantly work towards improving your skills, intentionally or unintentionally. In fact, as you continue working, your communication and leadership skills will improve significantly. It is because of these reasons that MLM is seen as a source of personality development as well.

DISADVANTAGES OF NETWORK MARKETING

❦

*N*ow that we have the advantages listed out, let us look at the other side of the coin as well. This section lists out all the cons that are associated with network marketing.

- *Complex Compensation Plans:*

THE MOST COMPLEX facet of MLM is the compensation plan. They are usually much more complex than they plainly appear in view of the fact that there are several details that you may miss out if you don't read the plan carefully.

- *Financial commitment:*

NETWORK MARKETING PLANS offered by some companies have details like hidden charges for brochures or CDs because of which the marketer may feel trapped. If you have fallen prey to one of these companies, you may end up paying a good amount of money to the company on a monthly basis.

- **Demands Extensive Motivation:**

ALWAYS REMEMBER the fact that MLM is synonymous with leveraged money. You are surviving on money that you earn from selling products or services of the company along with the sponsor commission that you get for the sales that your downlines get. While you can control and monitor your performance, it can be significantly difficult to monitor and control the performance of your downlines. So, MLM demands extensive motivation on your part to keep your downlines motivated and focused.

- *Severe Competition:*

IN VIEW of the fact that the entry to this business is rather easy to make, you can expect to face competition. You will really need to work hard to survive in this market.

- **Learn to accept rejection:**

YOU WILL BE FACED with rejection time and again. So, learn to live it and deal with it in such a manner that it motivates you to work harder.

NETWORK MARKETING SCAMS

. . .

NETWORK MARKETING IS all about numbers. The higher the sales, the better will be your profits. However, many companies use false numbers and statistics to woo people. One of the biggest reasons why people fear getting into this business is the fear of scam. Here are a few tricks that companies use to scam people.

- Money back guarantee schemes
- Portraying their products as magical solutions to people's problems.
- Upfront fee payment from distributors.
- Offering to give you downlines upon signup to start with.
- In some cases, no MLM Company may actually exist. So, they may just have a website.
- Asking you to buy products before signing up.
- Offering much higher commissions than the market rates.

In addition, the compensation plans of some companies may have tricky clauses that may find you in trouble later. The targets of these companies or any spam MLM Company are new marketers who are new to the Network Marketing world. Therefore, you must keep a check on what you are being offered and what is being demanded. You are the only guard you have against spams and frauds. So, beware!

ONLINE NETWORK MARKETING Opportunities

The objective of every network marketing company is to reach out to as many prospects as possible. However, efforts and time are usually the limiting factors. Therefore, you need to look for a plan that can help you reach maximum prospects in minimum time without having to invest efforts.

If there is one work that can give you the best answer to this question, then it is 'INTERNET'. Millions of companies all around the globe are investing in online multi-level marketing strategies to gain unprecedented competitive advantage.

Efficient Online Multi-level Marketing Guidelines

Given below are the guidelines to bring efficacy to any online multi-level marketing plan.

- *Create your Website:*

You cannot expect to get started with an online presence without a website. So, the first thing is to make a website and get it live on the Internet.

- *Attract Visitors:*

Regardless of how good your company and product/service are, all the goods will taste dust if your users or target customers are unable to access you or even know that you exist. Therefore, the second step is to advertise. You need to be visible and accessible to your target audience. There are several marketing strategies like viral marketing and sponsored ads that can be used for this purpose. If you talk in the context of the website, all you need to increase traffic to your website is to get search engine optimization done for it. This will improve your website's search rankings and your user base will gradually develop into unimaginable numbers.

- *Generate Leads:*

You have a website and you have visitors looking at it. You must be wondering as to what you will gain from this. You cannot gain anything substantial unless you convert your website visitors into business leads. In order to move forward towards your goal, you must ask your prospective customers for their contact information. You can use this information to contact your prospects individually later.

- *Building Relationship:*

So, now is the time when you will call your prospects and pitch in your product presentation to make an offer. This is the step where all the persuasion and convincing come into play. However, you cannot expect your customers to trust you with their time and money unless you have a bond of relationship with them. Building relationships online can be tricky. So, here are a few tips for you to help you build stronger and lasting relationships with your prospects.

TIP#1: *Give your customers value for money*

Your customers will never leave you if you are giving them value for their money and the best way to do this is to offer them nothing less than the best solution to their problem. Customer satisfaction is the biggest factor for retention. If a customer is satisfied with what he or she has got, he or she is sure to come back to you.

Remember that in MLM, you have to not just maintain a healthy relationship with your prospects or customers; you also need to maintain your equation with your downlines, immediate and others. The foundation of this relationship is support and trust. If you are able to help your downlines in their issues and conflicts and constantly work towards training them and making them better, you should be sharing a good rapport with them for sure.

TIP#2: *Brand yourself*

You can expect to face a lot of competition in the Network Marketing business. So, unless you set yourself apart from the crowd in the form of a brand, chances are that you will be lost in the crowd. Moreover, branding increases credibility and your prospects will trust you more of you are an established brand.

TIP # 3: *Stay in touch*

The secret to having long-term relationship with

customers is to never leave them. Your work doesn't end once you have sold the product. In fact, you can consider your work officially done once you have taken a feedback of how the customer liked your product. These tactics will help you retain your customers for the long run and ensure repeat sales.

TIP # 4: *Be positive*

Demands of the market fluctuate with time and as a sales representative, the market climate can be tough for you at times. In such times, do not lose hope and keep trying. Remember that if you lose your motivation to work, you will be the reason for your complete downline's failure.

TIP #5: *Generate sales*

Now that you have built a relationship with your customer, it is time for you to transform a prospect into a lead. However, with that said, never make the mistake of ignoring your repeat customers for new customers.

The guidelines discussed in this chapter shall help you achieve your targets and gain long-term success in your Network Marketing business.

AN OVERVIEW OF MULTI-LEVEL MARKETING

❦

*F*or any company that is hoping to generate profits and penetrate to the deeper levels of the market, multi-level marketing can prove to be a valuable asset. Regardless of your business, it is well known fact that you cannot hope to increase your profit unless you increase your sales. It is possible for companies to achieve their goals by putting MLM techniques into practice.

The best thing about the network marketing business is that it is a business of transformation. Consequently, in this business, everyone who is involved in the business around you is working to make your business grow. So, whether you succeed or not is completely up to you. It's all about the synergistic leadership. You need to create a business that facilitates and empowers rather than dominates and controls and its success is inevitable if it has strategies such as:

1. **COMPANY**: Company must be stable, strong and have a stable financial status.

2. PRODUCTS: Products should be differentiated and with unique qualities to offer.

3. PLAN: Should have a good compensation plan, which adds value to the life of distributors.

4. DEMAND: Product must be in demand in the present and the future market.

5. TIMING: Must not have been launched too long ago or must be in the period of growth

6. TEAM: Must have been a professional leader that can help you succeed

7. MANAGEMENT: The management must be professional and the administration must have knowledge in network marketing field.

COMPANY
    PRODUCTS
    PLAN
    DEMAND
    TIMING
    TEAM
    MGMT
    SUCCESS

It is important for you to remember that like for any other business, the network marketing business also requires you to put in consistent efforts and determined hard work. So, you cannot expect to get to your destination using some shortcut. However, if anyone tells you that MLM is a scam or is illegal, don't be fooled. MLM is legal, but you must be aware of all the fraudulent activities and their modes of working in your business.

Tips to Avoid Network marketing Scams:

- It is most crucial to do a thorough research of the company and the management that controls the same. You must have contact numbers, addresses and access to all the resources and people who hold important positions in the company. In case, you do not possess any of the information mentioned above, chances are high that you are being scammed.

- Before you join, be sure to go through the procedures and policies laid out by the company. In addition, before you sign the agreement, you must take relevant advice on reading and signing the agreements.
- Avoid lead generation systems that rely on friends and family
- Well, understand the compensation plan. It is important for you to know that if you are getting paid on the basis of the number of people that you hire, then this process of compensation is illegal. You must be paid for the sales that you or your subordinates are generating.
- It is important to investigate points like whether the company has up line support or not and if it believes in investing resources and funds in distributors training. If a company invests in training its staff, then it is sure to be a reliable organization.
- If the multi-level marketing company is asking for several hundreds or thousands to join upfront, there may be chances of being scammed.

All MLM firms are required to abide by the legal and ethical guidelines set for such organizations. Fulfillment of these conditions ensures that the firm will be able to persist the test of time and achieve success, in the long term. Another crucial dimension of MLM companies is the flexibility that they offer. This allows people to earn at their own pace. Finally, every multi-level marketer must keep in mind that earning money in this business requires persistent efforts and hard work. You may face some failure as you start, but these are just hurdles that you will learn to overcome. Just leave your failures behind you and move forward on your road to success and unimaginable monetary benefits.